Stations of the Cross for Young Catholics

Written by Sister Anne Flanagan, FSP

Illustrated by Gabhor Utomo

Nihil Obstat: Reverend Joseph Briody, S.S.L., S.T.D.

Imprimatur: ✠ Most Rev. Richard Garth Henning, S.T.D.
Archbishop of Boston
January 14, 2025

Library of Congress Control Number: 2025930572

ISBN 10: 0-8198-2765-7
ISBN 13: 978-0-8198-2765-4

This is a revised edition of the previously published *Children's Way of the Cross*.

Illustrated by Gabhor Utomo

Design by Daughters of St. Paul

Published by Pauline Books & Media, 50 Saint Pauls Avenue, Boston, MA 02130-3491

Printed in the U.S.A.

www.pauline.org

Pauline Books & Media is the publishing house of the Daughters of St. Paul, an international congregation of women religious serving the Church with the communications media.

1 2 3 4 5 6 7 8 9 30 29 28 27 26 25

Introduction

God had wonderful things in mind when creating people. They were made in God's image, meant to live with God's life, to make God visible in creation, and to share God's own happiness. Too bad that ever since the first sin in human history, people kept turning away from God in big things and little things.

So, in Jesus Christ, God came in person to tell us about true happiness and to show us how to live God's way. And when powerful people rejected him in the worst way possible, Jesus did something shocking. He suffered like an ordinary, powerless person. He did not work a miracle to escape. He did not shout people down. He did not blast his enemies to bits.

Jesus continued to show us how to live God's way, even in terrible suffering.

Jesus said humanity's great "yes" to God from the Cross. Jesus kept loving God his Father and all people under the worst possible conditions. He undid the "no" that had ruled over human history since the first sin. He took away the sins of the world: past, present, and future. Only Jesus could do that.

By his sacrifice on the cross, Jesus undid the effects of sin—sorrow, suffering and death—by experiencing them fully, and overcoming them from the inside. He didn't have to. He did it on purpose, for us. Through Jesus, God turned *everything* inside out, even bringing life out of his death by raising Jesus from the dead.

Jesus knows what it's like to face pain, sorrow, failure, betrayal. When you feel these things, you can bring them to Jesus. His rising from the dead is the promise that our suffering will not be the whole story. Saint Paul said that when you were baptized, you were baptized into Christ's death—so his resurrection is already in you, too.

And when you see people going through hard things, you will be able to treat them the way you would treat Jesus himself. Whatever we do for even the least important person in the world, we do for Jesus (see Matthew 25:40).

When Jesus lives in us, and we live like Jesus, God is at work changing the world!

How to Use This Booklet

For over a thousand years, people have walked the Stations of the Cross with Jesus. It is like making a pilgrimage, a holy journey, with him. You can pray the Stations of the Cross any time you want.

This book will help you pray with your imagination. That is not the same as daydreaming! In daydreams, your imagination takes your mind and heart to all kinds of silly (or sometimes scary) places. In prayer, you *ask the Holy Spirit to guide your imagination* in picturing a Bible story such as the suffering and death of Jesus.

All your senses can take part in this prayer. What do you feel? The uneven ground of the road or the marble wall you lean against? What do you see? Does Jesus glance your way? Look back at him and talk to him about what is happening. What do you hear? What do you smell? This is not pretending; this is *praying with your heart*.

The art in the book and the images in the church can help your imagination. If you pray the Stations on your own, you can take as long as you want with each one. You don't even have to finish the whole set.

If you are praying the Stations of the Cross with a class or group:

— The teacher or leader will ask different young people to read parts from the book.

— After Reader 2 finishes the "Imagine" section, there should be a short pause for prayer. The leader can let Reader 1 know when to begin the "Listen" section.

— Some members of the group might be asked to walk from station to station. They represent everyone else, following Jesus as he walked through the streets the day he died for us.

— Whether you have a special assignment or not, the important thing is that you pray, paying attention to Jesus in your heart as you recite the words, and using your imagination to meet Jesus and his mother Mary at each station.

OPENING PRAYER

(Stand)

All:

Dear Jesus, you died to save me; I am here to remember your great love for me. I am sorry for the times I have not returned your love. May these Stations of the Cross open my heart more and more to your gifts of love!

Holy Spirit, guide my mind and imagination as I follow in the footsteps of Jesus.

FIRST STATION

Leader:

First Station: Jesus Is Condemned to Death

Reader 1: Pray for people who cause others to suffer.

Leader: We adore you, O Christ, and we praise you.

All: Because by your holy cross, you have redeemed the world.

IMAGINE (*Sit or kneel*)

Reader 2:

Jesus' enemies captured him. They made fun of him all night. They really wanted to kill him, but someone else had to do it. So they brought Jesus to Pilate. You are there. You can see that Pilate is going to do what the crowd says. What do you want to say to Jesus as Pilate condemns him to death? (*Pause*)

LISTEN

Reader 1:

Christ himself suffered for you and left you an example, so that you would follow in his steps.

He committed no sin, and no one ever heard a lie come from his lips.

When he was insulted, he did not answer back with an insult; when he suffered, he did not threaten, but placed his hopes in God, the righteous Judge (1 Peter 2:21–23).

RESPOND (*Stand*)

All:

In my trouble I called to the Lord;
I called to my God for help.
In his temple he heard my voice;
he listened to my cry for help (Psalm 18:6).

SECOND STATION

Leader:

Second Station: Jesus Takes Up His Cross

Reader 1: Pray for people who are in pain.

Leader: We adore you, O Christ, and we praise you.

All: Because by your holy cross, you have redeemed the world.

IMAGINE (*Sit or kneel*)

Reader 2:

A big wooden cross gets laid across Jesus' shoulders. He will have to carry it for blocks and blocks. Let Jesus know that you are going to follow him the whole way. See Jesus take his first steps under the heavy cross. (*Pause*)

LISTEN

Reader 1:

Christ himself carried our sins in his body to the cross, so that we might die to sin and live for righteousness. It is by his wounds that you have been healed (1 Peter 2:24).

RESPOND (*Stand)*

All:

I praise you, Lord,
for being my guide.
Even in the darkest night,
your teachings fill my mind (Psalm 16:7 CEV).

THIRD STATION

Leader:

Third Station: Jesus Falls the First Time

Reader 1: Pray for the victims of violence.

Leader: We adore you, O Christ, and we praise you.

All: Because by your holy cross, you have redeemed the world.

IMAGINE (*Sit or kneel*)

Reader 2:

The crowded streets smell like dust and garbage. Jesus stumbles along with his heavy cross. Then he falls onto the dirty street, and the cross comes crashing down on him. He looks your way. (*Pause*)

LISTEN

Reader 1:

Jesus said to his disciples, "If any of you want to come with me, you must forget yourself, carry your cross, and follow me" (Matthew 16:24).

RESPOND (*Stand)*

All:

Please hurry, Lord,
and answer my prayer.
  I feel hopeless.
Don't turn away
  and leave me here to die (Psalm 143:7 CEV).

FOURTH STATION

Leader:

Fourth Station: Jesus Meets His Mother

Reader 1: Pray for people whose hearts are broken.

Leader: We adore you, O Christ, and we praise you.

All: Because by your holy cross, you have redeemed the world.

IMAGINE (*Sit or kneel*)

Reader 2:

Mary is following as closely as she can. Many long years before this, she had been told that her son would suffer. Run to catch up with her. Take her hand. It means a lot to her that you love Jesus, too. (*Pause*)

LISTEN

Reader 1:

[Simeon told Mary]: "This child is chosen by God for the destruction and the salvation of many in Israel. He will be a sign from God which many people will speak against and so reveal their secret thoughts. And sorrow, like a sharp sword, will break your own heart" (Luke 2:34–35).

RESPOND (*Stand)*

All:

Lord,
"With my own eyes I have seen your salvation,
which you have prepared in the presence of all peoples"
(Luke 2:30–31).

FIFTH STATION

Leader:

Fifth Station: Simon of Cyrene Helps Jesus

Reader 1: Pray for people who are treated unfairly.

Leader: We adore you, O Christ, and we praise you.

All: Because by your holy cross, you have redeemed the world.

IMAGINE (*Sit or kneel*)

Reader 2:

Jesus can hardly walk. So the soldiers pull a man from the crowd. "Carry that cross," they tell him. The man, Simon, doesn't want to get involved. Is there anything you can tell Simon? (*Pause*)

LISTEN

Reader 1:

God . . . will remember how you helped his people in the past and how you are still helping them. You belong to God, and he won't forget the love you have shown his people (Hebrews 6:10 CEV).

RESPOND (*Stand)*

All:

> But the Lord God keeps me
>   from being disgraced.
> So I refuse to give up,
> because I know
>   God will never let me down (Isaiah 50:7 CEV).

SIXTH STATION

Leader:

Sixth Station: Veronica Wipes Jesus' Face

Reader 1: Pray for people who dedicate their time to helping others.

Leader: We adore you, O Christ, and we praise you.

All: Because by your holy cross, you have redeemed the world.

IMAGINE (*Sit or kneel*)

Reader 2:

The dry sand, kicked up from the street, is getting in your eyes and nose. You can even taste the dirt. But you keep going. Up ahead, a lady pushes past the soldiers and wipes Jesus' face with a cool, wet towel. Aren't you glad that someone was so brave and kind? (*Pause*)

LISTEN

Reader 1:

"I was hungry and you fed me, thirsty and you gave me a drink . . . . I was sick and you took care of me, in prison and you visited me . . . , [W]henever you did this for one of the least important of these followers of mine, you did it for me!" (Matthew 25:35, 36b, 40).

RESPOND (*Stand)*

All:

They must thank the Lord for his constant love,
    for the wonderful things he did for them.
He satisfies those who are thirsty
    and fills the hungry with good things (Psalm 107:8–9).

SEVENTH STATION

Leader:

Seventh Station: Jesus Falls the Second Time

Reader 1: Pray for people who are discouraged.

Leader: We adore you, O Christ, and we praise you.

All: Because by your holy cross, you have redeemed the world.

IMAGINE (*Sit or kneel*)

Reader 2:

As the sad parade moves through the city, Jesus falls again. Look through the crowd. Is there anyone around who might give Jesus a hand? (*Pause*)

LISTEN

Reader 1:

If God is on our side, can anyone be against us? God did not keep back his own Son, but he gave him for us. If God did this, won't he freely give us everything else? If God says his chosen ones are acceptable to him, can anyone bring charges against them? (Romans 8:31-33 CEV).

RESPOND (*Stand)*

All:

The Lord is my light and my salvation;
I will fear no one.
The Lord protects me from all danger;
I will never be afraid (Psalm 27:1).

EIGHTH STATION

Leader:

Eighth Station: Jesus Meets the Good Women

Reader 1: Pray for families who are having problems.

Leader: We adore you, O Christ, and we praise you.

All: Because by your holy cross, you have redeemed the world.

IMAGINE (*Sit or kneel*)

Reader 2:

Is that the sound of crying? You turn to see a group of women coming near Jesus. Some men in the crowd start to make fun of the women, but Jesus gives them his attention. (*Pause*)

LISTEN

Reader 1:

Live in a way that is worthy of the people God has chosen to be his own. Always be humble and gentle. Patiently put up with each other and love each other (Ephesians 4:1-2 CEV).

RESPOND (*Stand)*

All:

The Lord will comfort his people;
he will have pity on his suffering people (Isaiah 49:13b).

NINTH STATION

Leader:

Ninth Station: Jesus Falls the Third Time

Reader 1: Pray for people who feel like giving up.

Leader: We adore you, O Christ, and we praise you.

All: Because by your holy cross, you have redeemed the world.

IMAGINE (*Sit or kneel*)

Reader 2:

This is taking so long—and there's still a way to go. You're not sure if you can make it. Jesus seems to be going even more slowly than before. He might not make it either. (*Pause*)

LISTEN

Reader 1:

[Saint Paul wrote:] I am happy about my sufferings for you, for by means of my physical sufferings I am helping to complete what still remains of Christ's sufferings on behalf of his body, the church (Colossians 1:24).

RESPOND (*Stand)*

All:

Please listen, Lord!
Answer my prayer for help.
When I am in trouble, I pray,
knowing you will listen (Psalm 86:6–7 CEV).

TENTH STATION

Leader:

Tenth Station: Jesus' Clothes Are Taken from Him

Reader 1: Pray for those who live in poverty.

Leader: We adore you, O Christ, and we praise you.

All: Because by your holy cross, you have redeemed the world.

IMAGINE (*Sit or kneel*)

Reader 2:

By the time you get to the hill called "Calvary," your clothes are sticky with dirt and sweat. Then you realize that the soldiers are going to make fun of Jesus by taking his clothes away. Before they reach him, you look into Jesus' eyes. What are they saying to you? (*Pause*)

LISTEN

Reader 1:

Can anything separate us from the love of Christ? Can trouble, suffering, and hard times? . . . Nothing in all creation can separate us from God's love for us in Christ Jesus our Lord! (Romans 8:35, 39 CEV).

RESPOND (*Stand*)

All:

I am weak and poor, O Lord,
  but you have not forgotten me.
You are my savior and my God—
  hurry to my aid! (Psalm 40:17).

ELEVENTH STATION

Leader:

Eleventh Station: Jesus Is Nailed to the Cross

Reader 1: Pray for people who have no one to help them.

Leader: We adore you, O Christ, and we praise you.

All: Because by your holy cross, you have redeemed the world.

IMAGINE (*Sit or kneel*)

Reader 2:

The cross is a mean and horrible way to die. How can people even do that to another person? How can they do it to Jesus? You see the huge nails and hide your face. Mary, the mother of Jesus, holds you tight. (*Pause*)

LISTEN

Reader 1:

This is how we know what love is: Christ gave his life for us. We too, then, ought to give our lives for others! If we . . . see others in need, yet close our hearts against them, how can we claim that we love God? (1 John 3:16-17)

RESPOND (*Stand)*

All:

The Lord doesn't hate
or despise the helpless
    in all of their troubles.
When I cried out, he listened (Psalm 22:24 CEV).

TWELFTH STATION

Leader:

Twelfth Station: Jesus Dies on the Cross

Reader 1: Pray for people who are close to death.

Leader: We adore you, O Christ, and we praise you.

All: Because by your holy cross, you have redeemed the world.

IMAGINE (*Sit or kneel*)

Reader 2:

You can't believe how long you've been here on this rocky hill. You squint your eyes to look up at Jesus on his cross. He looks back at you, but he can't say more than a few words at a time—to his mother, to John, to the criminal on the next cross. He is breathing very slowly. You are surprised to hear him call out to God in a loud voice.

The sky gets dark all of a sudden. Then everything grows quiet. (*Pause*)

LISTEN

Reader 1:

No one takes my life from me. I give it up willingly! I have the power to give it up and the power to receive it back again, just as my Father commanded me to do (John 10:18 CEV).

RESPOND (*Stand)*

All:

Even if I go through the deepest darkness,
    I will not be afraid, Lord,
    for you are with me (Psalm 23:4).

THIRTEENTH STATION

Leader:

Thirteenth Station: Jesus Is Taken from the Cross

Reader 1: Pray for people who have died.

Leader: We adore you, O Christ, and we praise you.

All: Because by your holy cross, you have redeemed the world.

IMAGINE (*Sit or kneel*)

Reader 2:

As the men take Jesus' body off the cross, you hear the big iron nails hitting the ground (and each other). An important-looking man hurries over with a long white cloth. No one is talking. Is there someone you can pray with? (*Pause*)

LISTEN

Reader 1:

All I want is to know Christ and to experience the power of his resurrection, to share in his sufferings and become like him in his death, in the hope that I myself will be raised from death to life (Philippians 3:10-11).

RESPOND (*Stand*)

All:

I am your chosen one.
You won't leave me in the grave
or let my body decay (Psalm 16:10 CEV).

FOURTEENTH STATION

Leader:

Fourteenth Station: Jesus Is Placed in the Tomb

Reader 1: Pray for people who live in fear.

Leader: We adore you, O Christ, and we praise you.

All: Because by your holy cross, you have redeemed the world.

IMAGINE (*Sit or kneel*)

Reader 2:

Everything is quiet except for the shuffling of feet as people carry the body of Jesus to a cave. You take one look back inside before the others push a huge rock in front of the entrance to close it off. The body of Jesus, wrapped with cloth, has been buried. It's time to go. (*Pause*)

LISTEN

Reader 1:

I consider that what we suffer at this present time cannot be compared at all with the glory that is going to be revealed to us. All of creation waits with eager longing for God to reveal his children (Romans 8:18-19).

RESPOND (*Stand)*

All:

But I will see you, because I have done no wrong;
and when I awake, your presence will fill me with joy (Psalm 17:15).

FIFTEENTH STATION

(Optional)

Leader:

Fifteenth Station: Jesus Rises from the Dead

Reader 1: Pray for people who need to find God in their lives.

Leader: We adore you, O Christ, and we praise you.

All: Because by your holy cross, you have redeemed the world.

IMAGINE (*Sit or kneel*)

Reader 2:

Why are people shouting so early in the morning?

What are the women saying? Jesus has been "raised"? What does that mean? (*Pause*)

LISTEN

Reader 1:

We know that God, who raised the Lord Jesus to life, will also raise us up with Jesus and take us, together with you, into his presence (2 Corinthians 4:14).

RESPOND (*Stand)*

All:

With his mighty arm
the Lord wins victories!
    The Lord is powerful! (Psalm 118:16 CEV).

CLOSING

(Sit or kneel)

Leader:

You have prayed the Stations of the Cross! It has been a real journey with Jesus, hasn't it? Now think back over the stations of the cross. Was there one moment where you seemed to meet Jesus and Mary in a new or important way? Call it to mind now. It is a gift from the Holy Spirit, just for you. Let the Holy Spirit warm your heart with that gift one more time.

(Pause for silent prayer)

PRAYER

(Stand)

All:

Dear Jesus, we have walked this way of the cross together: you, me, my friends, and all the people of the world. Show me how to keep walking with you and your people. Help me to share your nearness with others. Amen.

Sister Anne Flanagan, FSP, has been a Daughter of Saint Paul for over forty years. As a catechetical author and editor for Pauline Books & Media, she has "taught" tens of thousands of children. Her Eucharistic adoration guide for children, *Come to Jesus*, has been in print for almost ten years. Sister Anne has written for print, digital, and social media as a specialist in the spirituality of the Pauline Family, and she has recorded over two dozen albums with the Daughters of Saint Paul Choir.

Thank You!

When you read this book and share it with others, you help us in the work we do as Daughters of St. Paul. This book is part of our mission to communicate God's love.

We are praying for you!

Connect with us or send us prayer intentions at pauline.org.